Andruw Jones hits a home run in the 1996 World Series.

CONTENTS

Library of Congress Cataloging-in-Publication Data
Robinson, Tom.
  Andruw Jones : all-star on and off the field / by Tom Robinson.
    p. cm. — (Sports stars with heart)
  Includes bibliographical references and index.
  ISBN-13: 978-0-7660-2867-8
  ISBN-10: 0-7660-2867-4
  1. Jones, Andruw, 1977—Juvenile literature. 2. Baseball players—United
States—Biography—Juvenile literature. 3. Atlanta Braves (Baseball team)—
Juvenile literature. I. Title.
  GV865.J632R63 2007
  796.357092—dc22
  [B]   2006031919

Credits
Editorial Direction: Red Line Editorial, Inc. (Bob Temple)
Editor: Sue Green
Design and Page Production: The Design Lab

Printed in the United States of America

10 9 8 7 6 5 4 3 2

To Our Readers: We have done our best to make sure all Internet addresses in this book were active and appropriate when we went to press. However, the author and the publisher have no control over and assume no liability for the material available on those Internet sites or on other Web sites they may link to. Any comments or suggestions can be sent by e-mail to comments@enslow.com or to the address on the back cover.

Photographs © 2007: AP Photo/John Amis: 107; AP Photo/Scott Audette: 79; AP Photo/Shawn Baldwin: 64; AP Photo/John Bazemore: 1, 3, 10, 48; AP Photo/Charles Bennett: 3, 59; AP Photo/Roberto Borea: 4; AP Photo/Gary Dineen: 52; AP Photo/Ric Feld: 86; AP Photo/Lawrence Jackson: 103; AP Photo/Andres Leighton: 20; AP Photo/Mark Lennihan: 6; AP Photo/Erik S. Lesser: 44; AP Photo/Charlie Neibergall: 108; AP Photo/Chris O'Meara: 74; AP Photo/David J. Phillip: 81; AP Photo/Gene J. Puskar: 17; AP Photo/Ed Reinke: 85; AP Photo/Jeff Roberson: 110; AP Photo/Gregory Smith: 3, 98, 105; AP Photo/George Widman: 34; AP Photo/Mark Terrill: 57; AP Photo/David Zalubowski: 68

Cover Photo: Andruw Jones was one of many major-league players who used pink bats in games on May 14, 2006, to help raise awareness for breast cancer.

SPORTS STARS WITH HEART

Andruw Jones
ALL-STAR ON AND OFF THE FIELD

by Tom Robinson

Enslow Publishers, Inc.
40 Industrial Road
Box 398
Berkeley Heights, NJ 07922
USA
http://www.enslow.com

CHAPTER ONE

World Series Debut

T he World Series was back in the sport's most famous stadium—Yankee Stadium—for the first time in fifteen years when the 1996 Fall Classic opened. Andruw Jones, a teenager who was not even sure the Atlanta Braves would use him while trying to defend their world title, stepped into the batter's box in the second inning.

Just months after playing in Class A, three steps below the major leagues, Jones found a way to remain relatively calm while playing in front of 56,365 fans at Yankee Stadium and millions of fans watching on television around the world.

Jones watches his three-run homer in the third inning against the New York Yankees in the World Series opener.

Lefty Andy Pettitte, a 21-game winner, was working the mound for the Yankees with Javier Lopez on first base and the game tied. As he did so many times before his twentieth birthday, Jones produced a shocking performance.

He lofted a shot over the left-field fence, 388 feet from home plate. The shot, which produced an early 2–0 lead, allowed nineteen-year-old Jones to become the youngest player ever to hit a home run in the World Series. He broke the record set in 1952 by twenty-year-old Yankee great Mickey Mantle.

After Jones' shot, a celebration broke out on the tiny Caribbean island nation of Curaçao .

"It was an awakening," said Michaelangelo Celestina, who would go on to coach a team from Jones' hometown of Willemstad to a title in the 2004 Little League World Series and a second-place finish in 2005. "A total awakening."[1]

Fans poured into the streets, singing, dancing, shooting off fireworks, and beeping their car horns.

"It was wild," Celestina said, comparing it to the Fourth of July in the United States.[2]

> **"It was an awakening. A total awakening."**
>
> **—Michaelangelo Celestina**

The fans in Curaçao barely had a chance to catch their breath from Jones' first at-bat. The Braves put together another rally in the third inning and knocked Pettitte out of the game. They built the lead to 5–0 and had two men on base when Jones got his second chance to hit in a World Series. What would he do for an encore?

Incredibly, Jones sent the ball over the fence again. He hit a 380-foot shot into the left-field bullpen off of reliever Brian Boehringer. The shot broke the game open and gave the Braves an 8–0 lead on the way to a 12–1 romp in Game 1.

"We just left a couple of pitches up and he didn't miss them," Yankees manager Joe Torre said. "That's . . . an accomplishment for anyone in the World Series, not just a kid who's [just] come to the big leagues."[3]

Magda Rafael, Curaçao's sports commissioner, saw his country's reaction. By the time the World Series moved to Game 4 in Atlanta, Rafael had a giant television screen erected on the field at Willemstad's baseball stadium. Thousands of fans went to the stadium to

DID YOU KNOW?
Gene Tenace of the 1972 Oakland Athletics was the only other player to hit home runs in his first 2 World Series at-bats.

1996 WORLD SERIES
Game 1 in New York – Braves 12, Yankees 1
Game 2 in New York – Braves 4, Yankees 0
Game 3 in Atlanta – Yankees 5, Braves 2
Game 4 in Atlanta – Yankees 8, Braves 6, 10 innings
Game 5 in Atlanta – Yankees 1, Braves 0
Game 6 in New York – Yankees 3, Braves 2

watch on the big screen as the Yankees managed to tie the Series after losing the first two games.

"I've never seen the island react this way about anyone," Rafael said. He described Jones as "a true hero for this island's youth."[4]

The Yankees rallied to prevent the Braves from repeating their world title, winning in six games. Jones did all he could to help his team. He went 8-for-20 at the plate—a .400 batting average—and matched teammate Fred McGriff for the Series lead by driving in 6 runs.

SURPRISE APPEARANCE

Jones never expected to progress so far so fast. "I think it's really something special for me," he said after his back-to-back homers in the Series opener.[5]

When the playoffs started, Jones was pleasantly surprised to be on the Braves' twenty-five-man roster. He was not surprised when he sat on the bench for most of the divisional series victory sweep of the Los Angeles Dodgers. He drew a walk in his only at-bat.

Jones got more playing time during the National League Championship Series when the Braves rallied to win the last three games and beat the St. Louis Cardinals, four games to three. He gave a preview to his World Series performance by hitting a home run, which made him the youngest player ever to hit one in any playoff game.

Jones celebrates with his teammates after a win.

With the Yankees featuring three left-handed pitchers, Atlanta manager Bobby Cox decided to turn to Jones early in the World Series in place of Ryan Klesko. The left-handed hitting Klesko had trouble hitting against some tough left-handed pitchers.

Jones made the most of his chance and rewarded Cox for having confidence in his youngest player. "You don't treat him like a 19-year-old," Cox said.[6]

The fans in Curaçao did not treat Jones like someone who had just been on the losing team in the World Series. He was greeted by a parade when he returned home, and the whole island took part in the celebration.

IMPRESSIVE DEBUTS

By the time Jones put on his World Series show, he had made a habit of impressive debuts. In fact, the chance to hit the back-to-back home runs came about because of how well Jones responded to each chance to play at a new level.

No matter how highly regarded a young prospect is, it is very rare for him to climb up to the major leagues so quickly. It is even more rare for a teenager who had been competing in the Instructional League to rise up through the ranks of a World Champion team like the Braves.

"This is rarefied air he has moved in," Braves general manager John Schuerholz said. "But Andruw

ANDRUW JONES

Born: April 23, 1977, in
    Willemstad, Curaçao

Lives: Duluth, Georgia

Height: 6'1"

Weight: 210 pounds

Bats: Right

Throws: Right

Team: Atlanta Braves

Position: Center field

is a remarkable talent. He is unintimidated by his place on the baseball field."[7]

Jones signed with the Braves' organization as a sixteen-year-old on July 1, 1993. He reported to the team the next spring and spent much of the season with the Braves' team in the Gulf Coast League based out of the team's spring training complex.

When the Braves moved Jones out of camp to Danville of the Appalachian League, a higher-level rookie league, he went right to work. Jones batted .336 in 36 games.

Jones got to start the 1995 season by playing at Class A for the first time. There was no question he belonged. In the first ten games, he hit 7 home runs and drove in 18 runs. Although the Braves patiently kept him in Macon for the entire season, Jones was already on his way to the first of two straight Minor League Player of the Year awards. The next minor-league player award came for Jones' efforts over three levels on his way to the majors.

Baseball officials are used to watching players' statistical production dip when they go up to a new level. Jones' 1996 minor-league work showed the opposite, an improvement with each climb to a more competitive level.

After hitting .313 at Class A Durham, Jones hit .369 at Class AA Greenville and .378 at Class AAA Richmond. He did not even need an adjustment period. Less than a month after moving above Class A for the first time, Jones went on a 16-game hitting streak at Greenville. In his Class AAA debut on July 31, he went 3-for-5 with a home run and a stolen base.

HOW TO FIGURE A BATTING AVERAGE

- Andruw Jones had a batting average over .300, generally regarded as the mark of excellence, at each step of his minor-league career.

- Batting averages are determined by dividing hits by at-bats and expressing the result as a decimal carried out three places.

- Hits are how many times a batter hits the ball and reaches base safely without the help of an error by a fielder.

- At-bats are times that a batter comes to the plate, excluding walks, sacrifices, and sacrifice flies.

- For example, 7 hits in 25 at-bats is 7 divided by 25 or .280.

Jones had hits in ten of his twelve games at Richmond. During the last four games, he was 8-for-16 (.500) with 3 home runs and 9 RBIs. There was no longer any reason to hold him back.

"It doesn't take a genius to figure this out," Cox said. "He can play. He can really, really play."[8]

On August 14, 1996, Jones was called up to Atlanta. He made his debut the next day as the fourth-youngest player ever to appear in a game for the Braves. The day after that, Jones had his first major-league home run when he connected off Pittsburgh's Denny Neagle.

The 2 home runs in a World Series were a much bigger accomplishment, but Jones had his first 2-homer game as a major-league player just a week after he hit his first shot. All along the winding path of the 1996 season, Jones was helping convince Schuerholz and Cox that he could be trusted on an October night in the bright lights of New York City.

DID YOU KNOW?

Andruw Jones' home run in his second professional game August 16, 1996, made him the youngest National League player to hit a home run since Houston's Larry Dierker in 1965 and the youngest Brave since Bill Southworth in 1964. His 2 homers in a game less than a week later made him the youngest with that accomplishment since Danny Murphy of the Chicago Cubs in 1961.

"It's Broadway," Schuerholz said. "And that's where stars are born."[9]

The Braves had found a star they could rely on for the next decade.

CHAPTER TWO

Daring to Dream

Players on the Curaçao team at the 2005 Little League World Series were asked to name their favorite baseball players. Each answered, "Andruw Jones." Because Andruw did what was necessary to live out a dream that he shared with his father, Henry, young baseball players in Curaçao no longer had to think it was impossible to pursue the game in the United States someday.

"Andruw Jones gave this country a gift," said Zora Seferina, whose son Darren Seferina was one of the players on that 2005 Curaçao team that traveled to Williamsport, Pennsylvania. "He gave all these little kids the belief that a Curaçao kid can make it. He's the dream they have, he's the spirit that lights each one of their hearts. They listen and learn from every word he says."[1]

GAINING THE WORLD'S ATTENTION

The giant television screens that once brought Andruw Jones' World Series exploits back to his hometown fans in Willemstad get extra work in modern days. Baseball in Curaçao is no longer a secret, and when players from the country take to the world stage, the hometown fans like to be able to watch.

Curaçao sent a team to the Little League World Series five times, from 2001 to 2006.

Andruw Jones, the national hero who sponsors an entire Little League in his native land, had just finished adding to his major-league-leading home run title when he hit his forty-first and forty-second homers of the season in Milwaukee. The Atlanta Braves center fielder watched the Little League World Series on television with his teammates in the visiting clubhouse on August 28, 2005.

The Pabao Little League all-stars from Willemstad were trying to become the first team since Long Beach, California, in 1992–93 to win back-to-back world championships. Only a 7–6 extra-inning loss to Hawaii prevented the repeat.

"It's great to see," Andruw Jones said. "There's a lot of talent down there."

That talent is on display in four major leaguers, many more professional players in the minor leagues, and some of the best eleven- and twelve-year-old baseball players in the world.

Curaçao fans celebrated in 2004 when the Pabao team went 6–0 at the Little League World Series, taking the championship game, 5–2, from Conejo Valley of Thousand Oaks, California.

Carlos "Big Papi" Pineda batted .700 with 3 homers and 6 RBIs in the 5 games leading to the final, where he was the winning pitcher. People all around the world were watching the country's latest young baseball stars.

Carlos Pineda pitches for the Caribbean during the Little League World Series.

Henry Jones was one of the best baseball players of his generation living on the tiny Caribbean island nation. However, he grew up during a time when the dream of playing the game in the United States was not so realistic.

When Andruw was born, Curaçao did not yet have T-ball. When Andruw first joined his father to swing a baseball bat on a dusty field near his home in Willemstad, no Curaçao-born player had ever signed a contract to play professional baseball. Henry Jones did not let that stop little Andruw from talking about playing baseball in the United States someday.

ABOUT CURAÇAO

ALSO KNOWN AS: The nation is part of the Netherlands Antilles, or Dutch Antilles. There are five islands in the Netherlands Antilles—Saba, Sint Eustatius, and Sint Maarten in the north and Bonaire and Curaçao in the south.

PRONOUNCED: "Cure-a-sow"

LOCATION: Curaçao is in the southwestern Caribbean between Aruba and Bonaire, about thirty-five miles (fifty-six kilometers) off the northern coast of Venezuela.

SIZE: Curaçao is thirty-eight miles (sixty-one km) long. Its width varies, generally between two and seven miles [three and eleven km].

CAPITAL: Willemstad

POPULATION: Approximately 150,000

LANGUAGES: Dutch is the official language, but many on the island also speek Papiamento, English, and Spanish.

Andruw would go to his father's games and practices when Henry still played. He would stand among the best local players catching fly balls and telling them that some day he would be playing baseball in the United States.

"My dad is always telling me about the great players, and I have seen them," Andruw said. "I was always around them, and I know if I do well, it makes all of them happy."[2]

> **"My dad is always telling me about the great players, and I have seen them. I was always around them, and I know if I do well it makes all of them happy."**
>
> **—Andruw Jones**

With his father's teaching, it was not long before Andruw stood out on the baseball field. When he was only eleven, Andruw was selected for a youth team that traveled to Japan to play in a tournament.

Andruw's strong arm was apparent from the time he was of Little League age. He often played third base or catcher and showed off that arm before eventually making the move to center field.

19

Sidney de Jong of Team Netherlands in the World Baseball Classic

Henry Jones coached the Royal Scorpions, a team made up mostly of older teenagers, but his thirteen-year-old son was the one who often had people talking. One of the stories often repeated around Curaçao is about the day that summer when Andruw hit a home run about four hundred feet (one hundred twenty-two meters) onto the tennis court of the Holiday Beach Hotel. Then, as an encore, Andruw hit the ball over the tennis court and off the front wall of the hotel.

CHANGING TIMES

MAJOR LEAGUERS FROM CURAÇAO
Hensley Meulens
Andruw Jones
Randall Simon

Hensley Meulens broke through and, in 1985, became the first player from Curaçao to sign a professional baseball contract with a team in the United States. Andruw was eight years old at the time. As Andruw grew up, players from Latin American countries were becoming more and more prominent on major-league teams and in their farm systems.

The thirteen-year-old Andruw, who dominated against players sixteen to eighteen years old, grew into a fifteen-year-old who was regarded as the best player on the island.

A BRAVE DISCOVERY

Giovanni Viceisza, a part-time scout for the Atlanta Braves, saw Andruw play in a tournament in Puerto Rico when he was still fifteen. Viceisza began offering invitations to tryouts, but Andruw resisted.

Viceisza was telling the men he reported to that Andruw had to be seen. "Our part-time scout there, Giovanni Viceisza, had called our international scout, Bill Clark, who went down to look at him and then I went to see him," said Paul Snyder, the Braves' director of scouting and player development.[3]

Andruw's father was right by his side, running nearly stride for stride with him when the Braves began taking a closer look. Snyder lined up Andruw, Henry, and a speedy professional player who was already playing in the Braves' farm system. "We ran them sidesaddle standing start, as if they were breaking after taking a lead off first base," Snyder said. "The kid in our system ran the 60 in 6.53 (seconds) while Andrew ran 6.76 and his father ran 7.16. In a step and a half, Andrew was at full speed."[4]

If the Braves had any reason to wonder what kind of athlete Andruw was about to become, it certainly did not hurt that his forty-six-year-old father ran a respectable time and stayed close to his talented son and a professional athlete.

Henry had missed his chance to be discovered, but his son was not going to be overlooked. The Braves even had reason to be worried that other teams would see what they saw and start a bidding war for Andruw.

Snyder still needed to see Andruw play in a live game, but he did so without a stopwatch and notebook so that he would not stand out as a scout. Andruw's athletic ability continued to amaze the man who makes a living assessing young baseball talent.

DID YOU KNOW?
Andruw Jones' father, Henry, taught him to swing a sledgehammer with a short handle to strengthen his wrists. Andruw did this to build up his arms as a teenager and continued the routine into his professional career.

"On a single, Andruw rounded first base and put on the brakes, but never lost his balance," Snyder said. "I hadn't seen anybody do it that gracefully since I once saw Roberto Clemente do it against the Phillies in old Shibe Park."[5] Snyder left Curaçao with visions of Clemente, the late Hall of Famer, who came out of Nicaragua to reach stardom with the Pittsburgh Pirates.

Baseball rules prevented the Braves from doing anything yet. The following summer, on July 1 of the year Andruw was sixteen, the Braves signed him to a

> **"I think anybody who was playing baseball and really loved playing baseball wanted to play in the U.S., but no one was here to see. I watch Jones, and it makes me happy to see him playing so well."**
>
> **—Cedric Kirindongo**

professional contract on the first day they were legally allowed to do so.

Atlanta's willingness to take a closer look changed life for Curaçao athletes forever. Curaçao youngsters still play on fields with little or no grass because of the soil and saltwater conditions in the island nation. But on those fields, the youngsters know that the best among them will not be ignored. And the men who watch over baseball on the island take pride in what Andruw has accomplished.

"It was our dream, too," said Cedric Kirindongo, the sports editor of the Papiamento newspaper *La Prensa*. "I think anybody who was playing baseball and really loved playing baseball wanted to play in the U.S., but no one was here to see. I watch Jones, and it makes me happy to see him playing so well."[6]

CHAPTER THREE

On the Way

3

Following his dream meant Andruw would have to leave high school just before his seventeenth birthday. His education and international trips playing baseball had helped prepare him. Andruw headed for a new country knowing how to speak English, Spanish, Dutch, and Papiamento, an island dialect that combines the other three languages.

Andruw was one of many talented young players who gathered in West Palm Beach that spring. "He's a bright kid," said Paul Snyder, the Braves' director of scouting and player development. "He was planning to be an airplane mechanic until he found out that major-league players make more money. We were still projecting him then because you never know about kids no matter how much talent they have. Some level off. Some don't want it as bad."[1]

George Lombard, a two-sport standout whom many football fans had been planning on seeing play at the University of Georgia, was one of the most watched players from the first group of professionals with which Andruw played. Lombard immediately knew Andruw was the best of the pack. "He's the best player I've ever seen," Lombard said. "He's always been—even at 16, he was that good."[2]

ANDRUW JONES' MINOR-LEAGUE TEAMMATES

Gulf Coast Braves – Bruce Chen, Wes Helms, George Lombard, Fernando Lunar

Danville – Kevin Millwood, John Rocker

Macon – Wes Helms, Fernando Lunar, Kevin Millwood, John Rocker

Durham – Wes Helms, Kerry Ligtenberg, Kevin Millwood, John Rocker

Greenville – Randall Simon

Richmond – Jermaine Dye, Damon Hollins, Rod Nichols, Jason Schmidt

The recognition from others started before long. Although he did not put up particularly impressive numbers playing with the Gulf Coast Braves, based out of the team's spring-training complex in West Palm Beach, Andruw was moved up to another rookie league team in Danville, Virginia, midway through the season. At Danville, Andruw took off. He showed the speed he had used to impress scouts back in Curaçao. He stole 16 bases in 36 games while batting .336. When the first season ended, *Baseball America* magazine named Andruw one of the top ten prospects in all of minor-league baseball.

Baseball America is regarded as the authority on minor-league baseball. When Andruw was done with the 1995 season, his first full year of professional baseball, both *Baseball America* and *USA Today* named him the Minor League Player of the Year.

THE BRAVES' FARM SYSTEM

Draft picks and undrafted free agents pass through as many as six levels of the minor-league system, also known as the farm system, on their way to trying to become Atlanta Braves.

Rookie – Gulf Coast Braves, Disney World, Kissimmee, Florida (West Palm Beach when Andruw was a minor-league player)

Rookie – Danville Braves

Class A – Myrtle Beach Pelicans

Class A – Rome Braves (Macon when Andruw was a minor-league player)

Class AA – Mississippi Braves (Greenville when Andruw was a minor-league player)

Class AAA – Richmond Braves

Andruw received those honors—and many others—in 1995 without ever moving above the Class A level and the Braves' South Atlantic League farm team in Macon, Georgia. As just an eighteen-year-old, Andruw, the league's Most Valuable Player (MVP), hit 25 home runs, drove in 100 runs, and stole 56 bases.

The combination of speed and power were convincing many others of what the Braves' scouts had seen when they watched Andruw on fields at home in Curaçao. "He just has so much natural ability," Macon manager Nelson Norman said. "There is something there that you don't see at his age. You look at him and you can see something there that other players don't have."[3]

"There is something there that you don't see at his age."

—Nelson Norman

Andruw knew he could get even better. Trouble handling professional breaking balls, a common problem for young hitters, kept his batting average down to .277. That was a respectable average, but it did not match the impressive numbers he put up in other categories.

A year later, as he was making his incredible climb to the major leagues, Andruw reflected back on the 1995 season. "Last year, if a pitcher didn't throw me

ANDRUW JONES' MINOR-LEAGUE STATISTICS

YEAR	TEAM	LEAGUE	LEVEL	G	AB	HR	RBI	AVG.	SB
1994	Gulf Coast Braves	Gulf Coast	Rookie	27	95	2	10	.221	5
1994	Danville	Appalachian	Rookie	36	143	1	16	.336	16
1995	Macon	South Atlantic	A	139	537	25	100	.277	56
1996	Durham	Carolina	A	66	243	17	43	.313	16
1996	Greenville	Southern	AA	38	157	12	37	.369	12
1996	Richmond	International	AAA	12	45	5	12	.378	2
Total				318	1,220	62	218	.302	107

KEY:
G=Games
AB=At-bats
HR=Home Runs
RBI=Runs Batted In
AVG.=Average
SB=Stolen Bases

my pitch, I swung at it anyway," Andruw said. "This year, I wanted to make myself into a .300 hitter. I'm more relaxed. I wait for my pitch."[4]

For those who watched Andruw emerge as the hottest prospect in minor-league baseball in 1995, it had to be hard to imagine that he would find ways to make such significant improvements so quickly.

CHAPTER FOUR

Early Arrival

Andruw Jones was the reigning Minor League Player of the Year when spring training opened in 1995. He had never played at the Class AA or Class AAA level.

The Atlanta Braves decided to proceed cautiously and patiently. They never brought Jones into their major-league camp even for a look. The message seemed clear. At nineteen years old, Jones still had work to do with his fellow minor-league players.

The Braves started Jones in the Carolina League when the 1996 season opened. He was with a new team, but if there was a promotion involved, it was a subtle one from one Class A League—the South Atlantic League—to another. The traditional timeline in such a case would be to move the nineteen-year-old phenom up to Class AA at some point in the season.

Such a move would allow the player to reach Class AAA a year later, and, if progress continued, get a taste of major-league action as a September call-up when rosters are expanded. If more time was needed, there would not be a problem. After all, in that scenario, Jones would only be twenty the following September. He certainly did not need to be in the majors at that point to remain a prospect.

Jones may not have had a plan of his own, but his play on the field made any patient approach unnecessary. He started the year carrying a new label from *Baseball America*, this time as the number-one prospect in minor-league baseball. Jones fit that description perfectly.

BASEBALL AMERICA'S TOP 10 PROSPECTS FOR 1996

1. Andruw Jones, Atlanta Braves, outfielder
2. Paul Wilson, New York Mets, pitcher
3. Ruben Rivera, New York Yankees, outfielder
4. Darin Erstad, California Angels, outfielder
5. Alan Benes, St. Louis Cardinals, pitcher
6. Derek Jeter, New York Yankees, shortstop
7. Karim Garcia, Los Angeles Dodgers, outfielder
8. Livan Hernandez, Florida Marlins, pitcher
9. Vladimir Guerrero, Montreal Expos, outfielder
10. Ben Davis, San Diego Padres, catcher

The only statistic that caused mild concern from 1995, Jones' batting average, was immediately improved. His minor-league average climbed from .277 in 1995 to .339 in 1996 despite the fact that he played almost half of the time at higher levels.

Jones left Durham, North Carolina, and Class A ball for good at the All-Star break after playing sixty-six games. He breezed through Class AA, staying for just thirty-eight games, then hardly had time to unpack his suitcase at the highest level.

After arriving in Class AAA Richmond on the last day of July, Jones was gone by the middle of August. He spent just twelve games at that level. Each time he took another step up the minor-league ladder, his batting average climbed.

Each time he moved a step closer to the major leagues, he made more of a case that his time had come. On August 14, 1996, the Braves called Jones to the major leagues.

HITTING STREAKS

Andruw Jones had two hitting streaks of at least fourteen games while in the minor leagues in 1996. He hit in 14 straight games at Class A Durham April 30 to May 15. In that streak, he was 21-for-55 (.382) with 4 homers and 9 RBIs. He hit in 16 straight games at Class AA Greenville July 13–29. In the second streak, he was a torrid 33-for-68 (.485) with 8 homers, 20 RBIs, and 7 stolen bases.

> **"Players of that level of ability, with so much natural, God-given excellence, move up at their own pace."**
>
> —John Schuerholz

"Players of that level of ability, with so much natural, God-given excellence, move up at their own pace," Braves general manager John Schuerholz told *USA Today* not long before making the decision to bring Jones to the big-league club. "It's not anything anybody maps out or plans."[1]

Nobody would have dared to create such an ambitious plan when the season started. But when Jones moved to Class AAA, Bill Dancy, the Richmond manager, could see that he was not going to have long to work with his new outfielder.

Jones went 3-for-5 with a homer and a stolen base in his first game for the R-Braves. It was already clear that Jones' long-term future was as a center fielder, but Dancy could see the possibility of Jones filling a more immediate need elsewhere. Preparing for the possibility of Jones playing in either right field or left field for Atlanta before the season was done, Dancy moved his new star around for the two weeks he was in Richmond.

Jones follows through on his first major-league hit, a ninth-inning RBI single against the Philadelphia Phillies August 15, 1996.

Jones credited patience at the plate for helping his batting average soar. He learned to wait for pitches that he had a better chance to handle. His home-run count also improved, to 25 in just 116 games, and he still managed to steal 30 bases. Jones said the additional home-run pop was the result of getting bigger and stronger. "I was 178, 179 (pounds) last season," he said. "Now, I'm 190."[2]

ATLANTA AWAITS

The Atlanta Braves had already turned to one outfield prospect, twenty-two-year-old Jermaine Dye, earlier in the 1996 season when right fielder David Justice hurt his shoulder. With Jones tearing up Class AAA, he had become the next outfielder in line for a promotion by the time Dye went out with a knee injury.

Jones was told to meet the Braves in Philadelphia on August 14. The promotion made Jones the first player since Philadelphia pitcher Pat Combs in 1989 to start the season at Class A and get promoted through Class AA to AAA to the major leagues in the same season. Jones joined the starting lineup the next day, driving in a run and throwing out a runner from right field.

The Braves returned to Atlanta the next day, and the hometown fans got their first look at the star of the future. Jones had a home run and a triple in his first home game. After one day coming off the bench for his first appearance in center field, Jones was back in the starting lineup almost every day in right field. Ten games into his major-league career, Jones had produced at least 2 hits in five games, including one that featured 2 home runs. He was batting .325 and was on a 5-game hitting streak in which he went 8-for-19 (.421).

Major-league opponents pay attention when young players make such an immediate impact. With the Braves in contention for another world title, Jones was being watched closely. Scouting reports produced plans for how pitchers could attack him.

Although Jones' defensive play was clearly outstanding, his hitting quickly tailed off. Braves manager Bobby Cox used Jones less often as the season came to a close. Jones finished in a one-for-22 slump that dropped his Atlanta batting average to .217 in 31 games. He was not sure whether Cox would include him on the twenty-five-man active roster that the Braves would use for the playoffs.

PLAYOFF TIME

The Braves decided to keep Jones on the active roster. Cox used him as a defensive sub during a first-round sweep of the Los Angeles Dodgers. Jones came off the bench to appear in all three games.

Jones' playing time gradually increased in the National League Championship Series (NLCS) against the St. Louis Cardinals. The Braves had to win games 5 and 6 just to force Game 7 after falling behind, 3–1, in the series with the Cardinals. When the Braves rolled into the World Series with a 15–0 rout in Game 7, Jones helped back up Tom Glavine's shutout pitching with a home run.

After Jones went 2-for-9 in the NLCS, Cox trusted him with a Game 1 start in the World Series. The back-to-back home runs meant he would stay in the lineup throughout the six-game Series that the Yankees rallied to win. The two home runs in Game 1 allowed Jones to drive in 5 runs, matching the most ever in a World Series game by a National League player.

DID YOU KNOW?

When Andruw Jones hit a home run in Game 7 of the National League Championship Series on October 17, 1996, he broke Mickey Mantle's record to become the youngest player ever to hit a playoff home run. Mantle had been twenty when he homered in the 1952 World Series. That stood as the record for the youngest player to hit a home run in a World Series until Jones connected again three days later against the Yankees.

NAMING NAMES

On the night of Jones' famous 2-home run World Series debut, New York Yankees great Joe DiMaggio threw out the first pitch at Yankee Stadium. Cox could not help but think about how the defensive plays he had already seen from his young center fielder reminded him of the graceful Yankees great.

> "He can do it all. He made some amazing catches during the season and he did them with such grace. When I saw Joe DiMaggio throw out the first ball Sunday night, I thought . . . about a catch he made in St. Louis that he ran about 60 feet to make and did it so gracefully."
>
> —Bobby Cox

"He can do it all," Cox said. "He made some amazing catches during the season and he did them with such grace. When I saw Joe DiMaggio throw out the first ball Sunday night, I thought, now I'm not comparing this kid to Joe DiMaggio. But I thought about a catch he made in St. Louis that he ran about 60 feet to make and did it so gracefully."[3]

Jones broke Mickey Mantle's records. He earned an award named after Hank Aaron when he repeated as the top Braves minor-league player and as the Minor League Player of the Year in 1996. He brought up images of Joe DiMaggio and Roberto Clemente. Jones was still a teenager, but he was facing the pressure of being compared to the players who established themselves as the all-time greats of the game.

"One guy in baseball 50 years told me Jones is the best player he's ever seen," Schuerholz said. "One guy in our organization, Paul Snyder, says he's the best player we've had since Hank Aaron. Willie Stargell says he reminds him of Roberto Clemente.

"Those are the early returns."[4]

The Braves had been to two straight World Series. They had Justice, Marquis Grissom, and Ryan Klesko set in the outfield with Dye trying to break in. Jones showed he was ready, too. Schuerholz hinted at what was ahead for the organization by avoiding trying to name who would play a year later. "We'll just have to see how the club is constructed," he said.[5]

CHAPTER FIVE

There to Stay

Five outfielders capable of being major-league starters—David Justice, Ryan Klesko, Marquis Grissom, Jermaine Dye, and Andruw Jones—all reported to the 1997 Atlanta Braves' spring-training camp in West Palm Beach, Florida.

Grissom and Justice were used to playing every day. Klesko led the team with 34 homers and wanted the chance to show that as a left-handed power hitter he was capable of playing against left-handed pitchers, too. Dye hit .281 with 12 home runs as a rookie while Justice was recovering from shoulder surgery. Jones, still technically a rookie because of his limited time as a major-league player, had already made history in the World Series.

Something had to give. Before long, it did.

Early in spring training, the Braves traded Justice and Grissom to Cleveland for center fielder Kenny Lofton and relief pitcher Alan Embree. Days later, they sent Jermaine Dye and pitcher Jamie Walker to Kansas City for outfielder Michael Tucker and second baseman Keith Lockhart. Schuerholz's hints about the team being constructed differently were now understood.

"Coming into spring training, I think everybody expected something to happen," Braves third baseman Chipper Jones said.[1]

By sending three outfielders away and bringing only two back, the Braves trimmed the group of potential starters from five to four. More room had been made for Jones to fit in as a full-time player.

Jones had some trouble at the plate throughout spring training. If the trades had not already been made to clear the way, he might have to step back to the minors. Instead, the Braves kept him on their roster to start the season. Jones came off the bench as a pinch hitter on opening day and made his first start in the second game.

> ## "Coming into spring training, I think everybody expected something to happen."
>
> **—Chipper Jones**

A CONTROVERSIAL TRADE

The Atlanta Braves took part in one of the biggest trades of the 1990s in order to reshape their roster. "This is a trade of enormous magnitude for two very, very good franchises" is how Cleveland Indians general manager John Hart described it. A large motivating factor was finding consistent playing time for rookie outfielder Andruw Jones.

In a controversial move early in spring training of 1997, the Braves sent starting outfielders Marquis Grissom and David Justice to Cleveland for Kenny Lofton. Although Lofton was an all-star center fielder and leadoff hitter, his contract status, with only one year remaining before he was a free agent, made his future uncertain.

Braves general manager John Schuerholz said he had conversations with manager Bobby Cox "about the makeup of our ball club." Although the move was not immediately popular, Schuerholz insisted it was the right thing for the Braves. "We don't have any misgivings at all about how we have restructured the makeup of our roster," he said. "Our physical roster, we think, has been improved."

In addition to giving up two all-stars to get one, there were questions about things that are difficult to measure. Grissom was an Atlanta native and popular team leader. Together, Grissom and Justice had the experience of playing in 76 postseason games.

Lofton fit in by adding needed speed to Atlanta's powerful lineup. He had averaged 65 stolen bases for the previous five seasons and was coming off his career-best season with a .317 batting average, 210 hits, 14 homers, 67 RBIs, and 75 stolen bases.

Grissom had batted .308 with 23 homers and 28 stolen bases in 1996. Although Justice was hurt much of 1996, he was an established star and had produced 40 homers and 120 RBIs in the 1993 season.

While freeing up a roster spot for Jones, the Braves also cleared some room in their budget to be able to re-sign pitchers Greg Maddux and Tom Glavine at the end of the season. The pitching rotation was perhaps the biggest reason why Atlanta stayed on top throughout the 1990s and into the new millennium.

Eric Young throws over Andruw
Jones for a double play.

There was no doubt that Jones could play defensively with the best in the game. He also showed that he had the speed and power to make an impact offensively. It was consistency on offense that the Braves needed to see in order to commit to their twenty-year-old outfielder.

After coming off the bench as either a pinch hitter or a defensive replacement in six of his first ten appearances, Jones started showing the needed improvement in his batting average. He reached base in 4 out of 6 plate appearances, with 2 hits and 2 walks in an April 14 game against Cincinnati. With hits in seven of eight starts, Jones raised his average from .200 on April 13 to .278 on April 28.

Jones went 6-for-10 with a walk and drove in 3 runs in a stretch of three straight starts from May 11 to May 13. Gradually, his playing time was increasing. Jones shared the starting right-field job with Tucker at the beginning. Six weeks into the season, they worked together on a memorable victory.

Alan Benes of the St. Louis Cardinals was one out away from a no-hitter on May 16 when Tucker delivered a two-out double in the ninth inning. Although the no-hitter was on the line when Tucker came to the plate, the game was destined for extra innings. Greg Maddux had shut out St. Louis for eight innings, striking out 9 while giving up 7 hits. While Benes was more spectacular with 11 strikeouts, neither team scored. Jones entered the game as a pinch hitter for Ryan Klesko and took over in right field while Tucker moved to left to replace Klesko. Tucker eventually had 3 of Atlanta's 7 hits and was in position to score the game-winning run when Jones beat out an infield hit in the 13th inning against reliever John Frascatore. In a game that featured a combined 33 strikeouts, three short of the National League record, the Braves won, 1–0.

WORKING OVERTIME

Andruw Jones had 3 extra-inning, game-winning hits during 1997, his rookie season.

In addition to his run-scoring single to break a scoreless tie against St. Louis in the bottom of the 13th inning on May 16, Jones came up with 2 winners in the 10th innings of games. Jones hit a 2-run homer off Trevor Hoffman to end an April 26 game and give the Braves a 3–2 win against the San Diego Padres. He also had an RBI single in the top of the 10th in Philadelphia September 25 to lift the Braves to a 3–2 win against the Phillies.

After getting 91 at-bats total in April and May, Jones got more chances at the plate when Lofton was bothered by injuries in the middle of the season. He had 78 at-bats in June and 107 in July, combining for 13 multiple-hit games and 10 home runs in that stretch.

Jones' production—and therefore his chances to play—dipped a bit in the final two months of the regular season, but he managed some impressive overall numbers. In 399 at-bats, Jones put up 18 doubles, 18

1997 NATIONAL LEAGUE ROOKIE OF THE YEAR

Scott Rolen was a unanimous selection as the 1997 National League Rookie of the Year, receiving all 28 first-place votes for five points each and 140 voting points. Andruw Jones finished fifth. Three points were awarded for second-place votes and one point for third-place votes.

Voting point totals:

1.	Scott Rolen, Philadelphia	140
2.	Livan Hernandez, Florida	25
2.	Matt Morris, St. Louis	25
4.	Rich Loiselle, Pittsburgh	22
5.	Andruw Jones, Atlanta	15
6.	Vladimir Guerrero, Montreal	9
7.	Jose Guillen, Pittsburgh	4
7.	Brett Tomko, Cincinnati	4
9.	Jeremi Gonzalez, Chicago	3
9.	Tony Womack, Pittsburgh	3
11.	Kevin Orie, Chicago	1
11.	Neifi Perez, Colorado	1

Jones is all smiles in the outfield before the start of Game 2 of the World Series in New York October 21, 1996.

home runs, and 70 RBIs. Getting on base 58 times with walks helped make his .231 batting average a bit more acceptable.

Even when he did not start, Jones was often put in to help protect a lead because he was the team's best defensive outfielder. At other times, he was used as a pinch hitter. As a result, he appeared in 153 of 162 games.

The lineup changes had not hurt the Braves. They finished 101–61, the best record in the National League and nine games better than the second-place Florida Marlins in the East Division.

In the divisional playoff series sweep of the Houston Astros, Jones started just once and did not have a hit in 5 at-bats. He fared better in the National League Championship Series, going 4-for-9 in five games, but the Braves were eliminated by the Marlins.

The season ended in disappointment when the Braves outhit and outscored the Marlins and even had 6 home runs to one by Florida. None of that mattered when the Marlins pulled off an upset in six games. Florida took the lead in the series when Livan Hernandez struck out 15 to outduel Maddux, 2–1, in Game 5. One game later, Atlanta's season was done.

CHAPTER SIX

Defensive Whiz

The Atlanta Braves made room for Andruw Jones in the lineup and won more games than any team in the National League in 1997. With the 1998 season approaching, it was time to make room for Jones again—in center field.

Jones' powerful arm, his speed, and the instincts that allowed him to comfortably glide under fly balls that other outfielders could not reach added up to make him one of baseball's finest defensive outfielders. Although a strong arm is appreciated in right field, baseball teams put their best overall defensive outfielders in center field, the most important outfield spot defensively.

Kenny Lofton had been an all-star for four straight years and was a four-time Gold Glove winner as one of his league's three best defensive outfielders.

Still, the Braves let Jones leave as a free agent, once again thinning their crowded outfield and making it a better fit for Jones.

Jones had started forty games in center field in 1997, most of them when Lofton was out with a pulled groin from June 6 to July 28. Now, he moved into the position full time and did not leave. A year after being tied for third in the National League in outfield assists with 15, Jones was responsible for more than throwing out base runners. He was now the centerpiece of Atlanta's outfield.

DID YOU KNOW?
Once Andruw Jones moved into center field to start the 1998 season, that was the only position for him. From the start of the 1998 season through the end of the 2005 season, all 1,265 of Jones' defensive appearances were as a center fielder.

Atlanta's pitching staff has been famous—and for good reason—throughout the Braves' streak of division championships. However, pitchers such as Greg Maddux, Tom Glavine, and John Smoltz have had some help. Good defenses are built up the middle, and Jones handles the middle of the outfield.

Jones consistently turns more balls into outs than any other outfielder in the game. Jones' defense is well respected throughout baseball.

Jones slides safely into third base against the Brewers.

In that first year as a center fielder, Jones won his own Gold Glove. He has won one every year since. Maddux has said in interviews that Jones' defensive play saves every starting pitcher on the team about ten runs per year. When Jones made it nine straight Gold Gloves in 2006, only four outfielders in baseball history had been honored for their fielding more often.

OUTFIELDERS WITH THE MOST GOLD GLOVES

Roberto Clemente	12
Willie Mays	12
Ken Griffey	10
Al Kaline	10
Andruw Jones	9
Paul Blair	8
Barry Bonds	8
Andre Dawson	8
Jim Edmonds	8
Dwight Evans	8
Garry Maddox	8

RANGE FACTOR

Baseball is a sport famous for its statistics, but most of them have to do with hitting and pitching. Many fans of the game can recognize a good batting average, an impressive home run total, or an effective earned run average.

Defense is a little harder to describe statistically, and often an attempt is not even made. Committing the fewest errors is an important task, but there is much more to defense. Infielders need the ability to turn a double play. Outfielders can help their team with assists that are credited for throwing out base runners.

The most basic responsibility of a defensive player, however, is not always discussed. As a center fielder, Jones' most important job is to get to as many fly balls as possible. He does it as well as just about anybody in the history of the game. "I have never seen a center fielder run a ball down the way he can," San Francisco Giants slugger Barry Bonds said.[1]

An outfielder receives a putout when he catches a flyball. Jones has collected 400 or more putouts in five different seasons.

For people who seriously study baseball statistics, "range factor" is the category often used to describe the best defensive players. It combines putouts, assists, and errors to show how many balls a player gets to in a typical nine-inning game.

Different positions see a different number of chances in a typical game. Year after year, Jones has the range to get to more balls than other center fielders. As a rookie in 1997, he handled 2.58 chances per 9 innings in center field, compared to 2.03 for the rest of the league. In 1999, Jones handled 3.12 chances per game, compared to 2.20 for the rest of the league.

That extra .92 outs per game translates into one hundred forty-nine more outs for his team's defense each year compared to other center fielders. It is

ANDRUW JONES' DEFENSIVE STATISTICS

YEAR	POSITION	GAMES PLAYED	ASSISTS	ERRORS	FIELDING PERCENTAGE	RANGE FACTOR
1996	RF	20	4	2	.964	2.70
1996	CF	12	0	0	1.000	1.92
1997	RF	95	7	5	.969	1.63
1997	CF	57	8	2	.987	2.58
1997	LF	2	0	0	1.000	0.50
1998	CF	159	20	2	.995	2.72
1999	CF	162	13	10	.981	3.12
2000	CF	161	9	2	.996	2.78
2001	CF	161	10	6	.987	2.93
2002	CF	154	5	3	.993	2.66
2003	CF	155	8	3	.993	2.57
2004	CF	154	10	3	.993	2.59
2005	CF	159	11	2	.995	2.36
2006	CF	153	4	2	.995	2.61

Jones connects for an RBI single against the San Diego Padres in Game 5 of the National League Championship Series October 12, 1998.

therefore no wonder that Maddux suggested Jones saved the pitchers so many runs in a season.

Jones is not always so far ahead of the rest of the league, but he has been at 2.36 or better every year, while the league average has never been higher than 2.26. His worst season defensively is still far better than the best season for an average National League center fielder.

7 Everyday Player

ate in the summer of 2001, with his back feeling sore from the wear and tear of baseball's everyday grind, Andruw Jones left the Atlanta Braves lineup—for three innings. Those three innings were all that Jones sat out for the entire season. By then, manager Bobby Cox already knew he could pencil Jones' name into the lineup as the center fielder every day.

Once he took over the center field position in 1998, Jones was there to stay. He played all 162 games of the 1999 season, making him just the third Atlanta player ever to do so. Then, he went all the way until August 27, 2000, before having his consecutive-game streak end at 301 so that he could rest sore legs. When he took the day off on August 27 of that season, Jones

Jones makes a diving catch to rob the Chicago Cubs' Ron Coomer of a hit September 7, 2001.

had played every inning for the Braves since the season opened on April 3. The 301-game streak was the second longest in the major leagues. Only Sammy Sosa boasted a longer streak at the time.

With Lofton gone, twenty-one-year-old Jones was in center field for 159 games, all but three, of the 1998 season.

ESTABLISHING HIMSELF

Jones started out that 1998 season 0-for-14 in 4 starts and one pinch hitting appearance. His batting average never reached .200 until a 3-for-5 effort in Arizona April 28. From there, Jones used an 11-game hitting streak to bat .317 during May and get started on his way to more groundbreaking performances for such a young player.

Javy Lopez and Jones hit back-to-back home runs off Montreal's Mike Johnson in the third inning of a game June 13. In the next inning, Lopez and Jones did it again, becoming only the nineteenth teammates in baseball history to hit back-to-back homers twice in the same game. They erased a 4–0 first-inning deficit and put the Braves ahead, 7–4, on the way to a 9–7 victory.

There were some lessons to be learned along the way, however. Cox took Jones out of the game in the middle of an inning in July when the manager thought he was not hustling enough in the outfield. Jones responded to the embarrassing situation, giving the manager the effort he was looking for while making himself a key part of a team that won 106 games.

Jones already had 22 home runs on the season when he stole his twentieth base August 26 in a 6–2 win in Houston. Jones broke Cesar Cedeno's record as the youngest player ever to reach twenty in both categories in the same season. Jones finished his best month of the season with a .308 average, 8 home runs, and 10 stolen bases. He even stole home on August 31 against the Astros.

Jones led the Braves with 33 doubles, hit 31 home runs, stole 27 bases, and threw out 20 runners from the outfield.

When the Braves opened the playoffs against the Chicago Cubs, Jones did not have a hit in the series, but he did make contributions to the three-game sweep. He drew 3 walks, stole 2 bases, and scored twice.

DID YOU KNOW?

When Andruw Jones hit his fiftieth career home run September 6, 1998, in a 4–0 win against the New York Mets, he became the third-youngest player in history to reach that mark. Only Mel Ott and Tony Conigliaro got to fifty home runs at a younger age. Jones was twenty-one years and less than five months old at the time.

Jones' third-inning home run off Andy Ashby produced the first run of the National League Championship Series. He came through again with a sacrifice fly in the bottom of the ninth to drive in Atlanta's other run, but the San Diego Padres rallied to win, 3–2, in 10 innings. The Padres went on to win the series in six games.

Following the season, Jones returned to international play. He traveled with a team of Major League Baseball all-stars to play in Japan.

IRONMAN

The 1999 season was the first in which Jones played every game. He again struggled at the start of the season.

Jones had hits in five of his first ten games and took a .156 batting average into an April 18 game in Colorado. Any talk of an early-season slump ended that night as Jones and the rest of the Braves pounded the Rockies. The Braves set an Atlanta record for runs scored in a game in a 20–5 victory. Jones had 5 of the team's 24 hits. He went 5-for-6 with a triple, a home run, and 6 RBIs.

ANDRUW JONES HAD 6 GAME-WINNING HITS IN ATLANTA'S FINAL AT-BATS DURING THE 1999 SEASON:

Arizona, April 9 – RBI single in 10th inning for 3–2 win.

Arizona, April 11 – Two-run single in bottom of ninth inning for 3–2 win.

Pittsburgh, April 28 – RBI single in bottom of ninth for 5–4 win.

At San Francisco, May 11 – RBI single in 12th inning of 9–8 win.

Tampa Bay, June 9 – RBI single in 12th inning of 4–3 win.

At New York Yankees, July 16 – Three-run homer in 10–7 win.

While he was leading all major-league outfielders in putouts to claim his second Gold Glove award, Jones was also improving at the plate. He was learning to take more pitches and draw more walks than ever before. Jones was also becoming the man the Braves could count on to pull out close games. He won 6 games that year in Atlanta's final at-bats.

The Braves had a close race with the New York Mets in the East Division. Atlanta went 103–59 to beat out the Mets, who won 97 games. The division title was rewarding for the team, which went through the season without first baseman Andres Gallaraga, who was receiving cancer treatment, and then lost Lopez, the catcher, to a midseason knee injury.

Jones' hitless streak in the National League Division Series (NLDS) had reached 0-for-20 over three seasons before he broke through in Game 2. He wound up with hits in each of the last three games as the Braves eliminated the Astros in four games.

The Braves again had to get past the Mets. Jones had made a name for himself as one of the most dangerous hitters in baseball on the first pitch of an at-bat. He showed that the lessons about patience were also sinking in during his most important plate appearance of the season.

Jones, who had not yet driven in a run during the NLCS, came to the plate in the bottom of the 11th inning of Game 6 with a return to the World Series on

Jones hits a game-winning homer against the Yankees.

the line. He had 2 hits and had scored 3 times already in the game, but the Braves needed him to find a way to drive in a run with the bases loaded and no outs.

Nearly four-and-a-half hours into the game, facing the Mets' eighth pitcher of the night and the fourteenth used by the two teams combined, Jones took the simplest path to victory. He drew a walk from Kenny Rogers, forcing in Gerald Williams with the game- and series-winning run.

New York's other team, the Yankees, was there to again ruin the World Series for the Braves. With the help of an extra-inning win in Game 3, the Yankees swept the Series with four straight wins.

MORE DETERMINED

Jones went 1-for-13 in the World Series, leaving him determined to make the improvements necessary to raise his game to another level. During the winter between the 1999 and 2000 seasons, Jones spent less time back home in Curaçao. He spent more time in Atlanta, specifically in the batting cage, using the time between seasons to make himself a better hitter.

Jones' laid-back style and confident attitude had at times left observers wondering if he worked as hard as needed. When questions came up, critics could point to that midseason 1998 game when Cox took Jones off the field defensively. The off-season workouts were done in private, so they did not receive the same attention. Braves hitting coach Marv Rettenmund, however, was impressed with the work ethic he saw.

"A lot of people don't see how hard the kid works," Rettenmund said. "He's always relaxed, and you can't change that, but he wants to work."[1]

Jones had always been an excellent fastball hitter. That was one of the reasons he often had success on the first pitch, as pitchers tried to get a strike to get ahead in the count. Once he was behind, and pitchers could be more deceptive, Jones tended to have trouble, particularly against curveballs and sliders.

"I knew that was a problem," he said. "I had a lot to work on. If it is just see the ball, hit the ball, I am fine. . . . But after that, I needed to work."[2]

> **"A lot of people don't see how hard the kid works. He's always relaxed, and you can't change that, but he wants to work."**
>
> **—Marv Rettenmund**

Through the end of the 1999 season, when Jones got behind in the count, his average slipped to .209. When he had two strikes, he slipped all the way to .165. During the 2000 season, Jones improved those numbers to .279 when behind in the count and .201 with two strikes.

"I'm a fastball hitter, and when they leave a fastball out over the plate, I am going to hit it," he said. "But if it's not a fastball, I can hit it, go to right. I make better adjustments now."[3]

Jones adjusted to the point where he made the All-Star Game for the first time in his career. He had a hit and an RBI in his All-Star debut at the midway point in the season. Jones went right back to work when the season resumed. When he was done, he had his best numbers to that point in his career in the key statistical areas. He earned a .303 average, 36 homers, and 104 RBIs.

When it came time to take that break on August 27, Jones' play gave little hint that he needed his first day off since September 15, 1998. He had at least two hits in half the games he had played in August.

YOUNGEST PLAYERS WITH 100 CAREER HOME RUNS

Mel Ott	22 years, 132 days
Tony Conigliaro	22 years, 197 days
Eddie Mathews	22 years, 292 days
Alex Rodriguez	23 years, 16 days
Andruw Jones	23 years, 63 days

Henry Blanco bobbles the ball as Jones slides into home.

Until Jones decided to sit out the game against the St. Louis Cardinals, he had been the only player in the major leagues to appear in every inning that season.

The season ended in disappointment with a three-game loss to the St. Louis Cardinals in the first round of the playoffs. Jones only had one hit in the series, and it was a home run.

LOFTY STANDARDS

Jones kept up his defense and power production during the 2001 season, hitting 34 homers and driving in 104 runs. His average slipped back to .251.

The Braves went through a similar season. They managed to keep their streak of division titles alive, but they needed some help from their division rivals after dropping down to just eighty-eight wins.

"I make better adjustments now."

—Andruw Jones

As the 2001 playoffs approached, Jones and the Braves as a whole had something to prove.

CHAPTER EIGHT

Playoff Upset

8

The Atlanta Braves often enter the postseason as one of the favorites to represent the National League in the World Series. As the playoff team with the least regular-season victories, the Braves were the underdogs as the 2001 postseason began.

Andruw Jones was also used to big expectations. After a few postseason struggles, however, there may have been just as many predictions of offensive struggles for Jones when the playoffs arrived in 2001.

Drop-offs in Jones' batting average and the Braves' win total meant uncertainty heading into a series against the Houston Astros. The Braves did not need long to change that. They eliminated the Astros from the playoffs for the third time in five seasons. Atlanta needed just three games to get through the first round.

ATLANTA BRAVES PLAYOFF HISTORY

YEAR	ROUND	OPPONENT	RESULT
1969	League Championship Series	New York Mets	Lost, 3–0
1982	League Championship Series	St. Louis Cardinals	Lost, 3–0
1991	League Championship Series	Pittsburgh Pirates	Won, 4–3
1991	World Series	Minnesota Twins	Lost, 4–3
1992	League Championship Series	Pittsburgh Pirates	Won, 4–3
1992	World Series	Toronto Blue Jays	Lost, 4–2
1993	League Championship Series	Philadelphia Phillies	Lost, 4–2
1995	Division Series	Colorado Rockies	Won, 3–1
1995	League Championship Series	Cincinnati Reds	Won, 4–0
1995	World Series	Cleveland Indians	Won, 4–2

- When the franchise was in Boston, it reached the World Series in 1914 and 1948. The Boston Braves beat the Philadelphia Athletics, 4–0, in 1914 and lost to the Cleveland Indians, 4–2, in 1948.

- The franchise also reached the World Series twice while located in Milwaukee. The Milwaukee Braves beat the New York Yankees, 4–3, in 1957 and lost to the Yankees, 4–3, in 1958.

- The Milwaukee Braves also lost, 2–0, to the Los Angeles Dodgers in a best-of-three National League tiebreaker playoff in 1959.

YEAR	ROUND	OPPONENT	RESULT
(With Andruw Jones on team)			
1996	Division Series	Los Angeles Dodgers	Won, 3–0
1996	League Championship Series	St. Louis Cardinals	Won, 4–3
1996	World Series	New York Yankees	Lost, 4–2
1997	Division Series	Houston Astros	Won, 3–0
1997	League Championship Series	Florida Marlins	Lost, 4–2
1998	Division Series	Chicago Cubs	Won, 3–0
1998	League Championship Series	San Diego Padres	Lost, 4–2
1999	Division Series	Houston Astros	Won, 3–1
1999	League Championship Series	New York Mets	Won, 4–2
1999	World Series	New York Yankees	Lost, 4–0
2000	Division Series	St. Louis Cardinals	Lost, 3–0
2001	Division Series	Houston Astros	Won, 3–0
2001	League Championship Series	Arizona Diamondbacks	Lost, 4–1
2002	Division Series	San Francisco Giants	Lost, 3–2
2003	Division Series	Chicago Cubs	Lost, 3–2
2004	Division Series	Houston Astros	Lost, 3–2
2005	Division Series	Houston Astros	Lost, 3–1

Chipper Jones watches his homer against the Astros in the National League Division Series October 12, 2001.

"It's extremely disappointing," Houston second baseman Craig Biggio said. "We really thought this time it would be different."[1]

Jones had a big role in making sure that when it came time for a Braves and Astros playoff series, some things never changed.

The playoff struggles were put in the past when Jones had hits in his last two at-bats of the opener. His home run to left field to lead off the ninth inning gave the Braves a 7–3 lead on the way to a 7–4 win.

Chipper Jones put the Braves ahead in the eighth inning with a 3-run homer to greet relief ace Billy Wagner.

Veteran left-handed pitcher Tom Glavine made sure the Braves took command with a second straight win in Houston. Glavine beat Houston for the twelfth straight time by working 8 scoreless innings, giving up 6 singles and 2 walks.

"I think that we've been in a situation against these guys where seemingly we've done everything we needed to

DID YOU KNOW?

Baseball's postseason consisted solely of the World Series until 1969. In 1969, the American League and National League each split into two divisions and held a League Championship Series to determine which team went to the World Series. The playoffs expanded again in 1995 when each league went to three divisions. The Division Series consists of the three division champions and the wild card, which is the second-best team with the best record in each league.

> **"I think that we've been in a situation against these guys where seemingly we've done everything we needed to do and everything's gone our way."**
>
> **—Tom Glavine**

do and everything's gone our way," Glavine said.[2]

Glavine did not need much support. Jones helped provide what was needed in the second inning. B.J. Surhoff was on second base with a leadoff double. Jones beat out an infield single, and Surhoff advanced to third on the play. When the Astros turned a double play, Surhoff came in and wound up being the game's only run.

Jones got hits in his first 3 at-bats of the game, tying a division series record with 5 consecutive hits. Marquis Grissom, Chad Fonville, and Tony Armas were the only other players to accomplish that feat.

Jones singled and scored on a Paul Bako suicide squeeze bunt in the series-clinching 6–2 victory.

The Braves could not keep up the momentum in the National League Championship Series.

Glavine pitched another masterful game, and Jones scored twice during an 8–1 win in Game 2, but that was the only victory of the series. The

ANDRUW JONES' CAREER PLAYOFF STATISTICS (BY SERIES)									
SERIES	YEARS	W–L	G	AB	R	H	HR	RBI	AVG.
NL Division Series	10	5–5	38	125	23	36	5	19	.288
NL Championship Series	5	2–3	27	80	15	20	3	8	.250
World Series	2	0–2	10	33	5	9	2	6	.273
Totals	17	7–10	75	238	43	65	10	33	.273

KEY:
W–L=Wins–Losses
G=Games
AB=At-bats
R=Runs
H=Hits
HR=Home Runs
RBI=Runs Batted In
AVG.=Average

dominant combination of Randy Johnson and Curt Schilling, which would go on to lead a defeat of the New York Yankees in the World Series, produced three of the four wins the Arizona Diamondbacks needed to end Atlanta's season.

Jones' homer off Albie Lopez was not enough in the other game. He gave the Braves a 2–0 lead in the second inning of Game 4, but they lost, 11–4.

FALLING SHORT

After winning the World Series once and reaching it four other times in the 1990s, the Atlanta Braves had trouble getting back in the new millennium.

The Braves played in nine out of ten NLCS from 1991 to 2001. None was held in 1994 because of the baseball strike. The 2001 upset of the Astros was the end of that run. Atlanta lost in the NLDS four straight times from 2002 to 2005. The first three of those eliminations came in the fifth and deciding game.

Houston began evening up the playoff history. The Astros eliminated the Braves from both the 2004 and 2005 playoffs.

ANDRUW JONES' PLAYOFF STATISTICS (BY YEAR)							
YEAR	G	AB	R	H	HR	RBI	AVG.
1996	14	29	7	10	3	9	.345
1997	8	14	1	4	0	2	.286
1998	9	31	5	6	1	3	.194
1999	14	54	7	10	0	3	.185
2000	3	9	3	1	1	1	.111
2001	8	29	6	9	2	2	.310
2002	5	19	4	6	0	2	.316
2003	5	17	1	1	0	1	.059
2004	5	19	4	10	2	5	.526
2005	4	17	5	8	1	5	.471
Totals	75	238	43	65	10	33	.273

KEY:
G=Games
AB=At-bats
R=Runs
H=Hits
HR=Home Runs
RBI=Runs Batted In
AVG.=Average

Jones laughs during batting practice in 2002.

Jones became one of the most reliable hitters on the playoff teams that came up just short. He batted .316 in the loss to the San Francisco Giants in 2002. After losing the first game, the Braves won two straight. Jones drove in 2 runs with a single in the ninth inning of a 10–2 romp in Game 3 to give Atlanta a 2–1 series lead. The Giants came back with two straight wins, including a 3–1 victory in the deciding Game 5.

The only hit Jones produced in the 2003 NLDS against Chicago was a single to drive in a run and force a 2–2 tie in the bottom of the fourth inning of Game 2. The Braves went on to win, 5–3, to tie the series. They also won Game 4 to come back and tie the series again, but the Cubs won Game 5, 5–1.

MOST CAREER POSTSEASON RUNS SCORED (THROUGH 2006 PLAYOFFS)

1. Derek Jeter	85
2. Bernie Williams	83
3. Kenny Lofton	61
4. Chipper Jones	58
5. David Justice	55
6. Rickey Henderson	47
6. Tino Martinez	47
6. Manny Ramirez	47
9. Andruw Jones	43
10. Mickey Mantle	42

OFFENSIVE LEADER

When the Astros finally got the best of the Braves in 2004 and 2005, they had to overcome huge efforts by Jones to do so. In the two series combined, Jones

Jones slides across home plate in a game against the Astros.

drove in 10 runs and scored 9 while hitting 3 homers and batting a combined .500 in 9 games.

With four strong playoff efforts in five seasons, Jones was one of the veterans the Braves counted on offensively in October.

Jones had hits in every game of the 2004 NLDS and more than one hit in three of the five games.

By the time Jones hit a two-out solo homer off Roger Clemens in the bottom of the fifth inning of the opening game, he could only manage to cut Houston's lead to 7–2. The Braves were in the process of matching a negative team playoff record by leaving twelve men on base during a 9–3 loss. Ten of the men who were left on base were in the first five innings.

> ## "We should have taken advantage when we had the opportunities. Unfortunately we didn't. That was the ball game right there."
>
> **—Andruw Jones**

"We should have taken advantage when we had the opportunities," Jones said. "Unfortunately we didn't. That was the ball game right there."[3]

The Braves won Game 2, 4–2, in 11 innings, but lost Game 3 despite a huge effort by Jones. The center fielder went 3-for-4, but his 3-run homer in the eighth inning could only cut the final margin to 8–5.

Jones came back with 3 more hits in Game 4 to help extend another division series to a fifth and deciding game. He scored a run and drove in another. The Braves came through with a run in the ninth inning for a 6–5 victory that ended Houston's nineteen-game home winning streak and sent the series back to Atlanta.

The Braves scored two runs in the fifth inning, cutting the Astros' lead to 3–2 and turning Game 5 into a battle of bullpens by knocking Roy Oswalt out of the game. Everything that possibly could go wrong from there did, and Houston advanced with a 12–3 victory.

Atlanta's playoffs ended in fewer games but just about as many innings in 2005. Houston won the series in four games with the clinching victory coming in an 18-inning game that was the longest in playoff history.

Chipper Jones got to Andy Pettitte for a solo homer in the first inning. Andruw Jones added a 2-run shot in the fourth during Game 1. Even then, the Braves were behind, 4–3, in what would become a 10–5 loss.

Andruw Jones had 3 hits and scored 3 times, and John Smoltz outdueled Clemens to set a record for postseason victories as the Braves bounced back with a 7–1 win in Game 2.

THE LONGEST GAME

Andruw Jones' best season came to an end with the longest playoff game in major-league history.

The Houston Astros and Atlanta Braves set a series of records during Houston's 7–6 victory October 9, 2005, to finish off the National League Division Series.

Jones did his part early in the game to give the Braves what seemed to be a comfortable lead. He was one of the runners on base when Adam LaRoche hit a third-inning grand slam for a 4–0 lead. His sacrifice fly in the fifth inning made the lead 5–0. In between, he made a diving backhand grab of a sinking Morgan Ensberg line drive. He grabbed the ball just before it reached the turf, ending the fourth inning in the process.

Houston's Lance Berkman hit a grand slam in the eighth inning, making it the only game in playoff history with two bases-loaded home runs and bringing the Astros to within one at 6–5. Brad Ausmus homered in the bottom of the ninth to force extra innings.

The teams remained scoreless for the next eight innings. Rookie Chris Burke then brought a sudden end to the game with a solo homer off Joey Devine in the bottom of the 18th inning.

Legendary pitcher Roger Clemens was the last available arm for the Astros. With just two days rest after his previous start, he came on to retire 9 of 11 batters while pitching 3 scoreless innings for the win.

Jones finished the game 1-for-6 with a walk.

Jones stands in the dugout in Atlanta October 4, 2005. The Braves would take on the Astros in the NLDS October 5.

The game lasted 18 innings, two longer than the previous record from a 1986 New York Mets and Astros National League Championship Series game. It took five hours and fifty minutes to complete, one more minute than the New York Yankees and Boston Red Sox needed in a 2004 American League Championship Series game. A total of forty-two players and five hundred fifty-three pitches were needed to complete the game.

Jones hits a homer off the Astros' Andy Pettitte.

For the fourth time in six playoff games over two seasons, Jones went out and got 3 more hits in the next game. Two of the hits were doubles, and one of those drove in a run, but Houston won, 7–3, to put Atlanta on the verge of elimination.

The Astros needed some extra time to finish off the Braves. After 18 tiring innings, they emerged with a 7–6 victory and continued on their way to the World Series.

CHAPTER NINE

Continued Dominance

Andruw Jones was standing in the on-deck circle at Veterans Stadium in Philadelphia when the Atlanta Braves were retired during the ninth inning of a 7–1 victory. On September 25, 2002, he did not get one last chance to hit and add to one of the biggest nights of his professional career. Jones had already made the most of the chances he did get.

After hitting 2 home runs in a game 10 times during his career—5 times that season and twice earlier that month—Jones broke through with the first 3-homer game of his major-league career. "When he stays on the ball, there's nobody better," Braves manager Bobby Cox said. "It's fun to watch him hit when he's right on."[1]

> "... It's fun to watch him hit when he's right on."
>
> —Bobby Cox

Jones hit solo home runs off Phillies starter Brett Myers to lead off the second and fourth innings. "He hit everything tonight," Myers said. "He was locked in. He was hitting good pitches and bad pitches."[2] After being retired by Hector Mercado in his third at-bat, Jones added a 2-run shot off Jose Santiago in the eighth inning.

Jones took pitches to three different parts of the strike zone and gave each the same destination—over the outfield fence. "The first at-bat, that pitch was kind of away," he said. "The second one was down and I had a good swing at it. The third one, I think it was a mistake. He tried to throw the ball in, and he left just a little bit over the plate."[3]

Although the 3-homer game was a first for Jones, the late-season outburst was not surprising. He had a big September in 2001 to help the Braves beat the Philadelphia Phillies by two games in a close race for the East Division title.

In 2002, he finished strong again while the Braves coasted to the finish with a big lead in the division.

The Braves faced many challenges along the way, but none stopped them from winning fourteen straight division titles from 1992 to 2005.

DIVISION TITLE STREAK

Year: 1991   Record: 94–68

Second Place: **Los Angeles Dodgers, 93–69**

Andruw Jones' Role: **Not yet signed**

Notable:

- **The Braves became the first team in National League history to go from last place to first place in one season.**

- **Tom Glavine won 20 games.**

- **The Braves signed free agent Terry Pendleton before the season, and the third baseman raised his average from .230 to .319 while winning the Most Valuable Player award.**

- **The Braves held the Pittsburgh Pirates scoreless for the final twenty-seven innings to win the National League Championship Series in seven games. A classic World Series ended when the Minnesota Twins took Game 7, 1–0, in 10 innings.**

Year: 1992   Record: 98–64

Second Place: **Cincinnati Reds, 90–72**

Andruw Jones' Role: **Not yet signed**

Notable:

- **The Braves started 23–27 but went 75–37 from June 1 to the end of the season.**

- **Tom Glavine went 20–8 to lead the rotation while Pete Smith filled in by going 7–0 with a 2.05 ERA.**

Year: 1993   Record: 104–58

Second Place: San Francisco Giants, 103–59

Andruw Jones' Role: Signed in the summer but did not start professional career

Notable:

- The Braves were ten games out of first place on July 22 but went 41–15 in the final two months and won the division on the final day of the season.
- Tom Glavine went 22–6 while Greg Maddux was 20–10 with a 2.36 ERA and won the Cy Young Award in his first season with the team.

Year: 1995   Record: 90–54

Second Place: New York Mets and Philadelphia Phillies, 69–75

Andruw Jones' Role: Still working his way through minor leagues

Notable:

- The Braves moved to the East Division when the National League realigned for the 1994 season, which was eventually shortened by a strike.
- Greg Maddux won his fourth straight Cy Young Award by going 19–2 with a 1.63 ERA.
- The Braves beat the Cleveland Indians in a six-game World Series.

Year: 1996   Record: 96–66

Second Place: Montreal Expos, 88–74

Andruw Jones' Role: Called up for the first time as a nineteen-year-old and filled in well enough in the outfield to make the playoff roster

Notable:

- John Smoltz won 24 games and the Cy Young Award.
- Mark Wohlers saved 39 games.

Year: 1997   Record: 101–61

Second Place: Florida, 92–70

Andruw Jones' Role: Hit 18 homers in his first full season with the team

Notable:

• **Braves had the best record in the National League.**

• **Denny Neagle went 20–5 with a 2.97 ERA.**

Year: 1998   Record: 106–56

Second Place: New York Mets, 88–74

Andruw Jones' Role: Made the move to become the team's everyday center fielder and won his first Gold Glove

Notable:

• **Tom Glavine, Greg Maddux, John Smoltz, Denny Neagle, and Kevin Millwood all won at least sixteen games.**

• **Andres Galarraga, Javy Lopez, and Chipper Jones all joined Andruw Jones with at least thirty homers.**

• **Chipper Jones was named MVP.**

Year: 1999   Record: 103–59

Second Place: New York Mets, 97–66

Andruw Jones' Role: Led major-league outfielders in putouts

Notable:

• **The Braves pulled away by winning five of six late-season games from the Mets.**

• **John Rocker set a team record with 38 saves.**

Year: 2000   **Record: 95–67**

Second Place: **New York Mets, 94–68**

Andruw Jones' Role: **Made the All-Star Game for the first time**

Notable:

- **The Braves won fifteen straight in April and May on their way to becoming only the third franchise in major-league history with nine straight 90-win seasons.**
- **Rafael Furcal was named Rookie of the Year.**
- **Tom Glavine led the majors with 21 wins.**

Year: 2001   **Record: 88–74**

Second Place: **Philadelphia Phillies, 86–76**

Andruw Jones' Role: **Drove in 104 runs for the second straight season**

Notable:

- **The Braves had to hold off both the Mets and Phillies in the final week of the season.**
- **John Burkett and Greg Maddux finished third and fourth in the league in ERA.**

Year: 2002   **Record: 101–59**

Second Place: **Montreal Expos, 83–79**

Andruw Jones' Role: **Led the team with 36 homers**

Notable:

- **Team ERA of 3.13 led league for ninth time in twelve years.**
- **Chris Hammond had an 0.95 ERA in 75 relief innings.**

Year: 2003   **Record: 101–61**

Second Place: Florida Marlins, 91–71

Andruw Jones' Role: Reached a new career high with 116 RBIs

Notable:

• **The Braves went on a 60–20 tear, beginning May 15.**

• **When they clinched on September 9, it was the earliest in team history.**

Year: 2004   **Record: 96–66**

Second Place: Philadelphia Phillies, 86–76

Andruw Jones' Role: Earned his seventh straight Gold Glove award

Notable:

• **The Braves led the National League in ERA for the tenth time in thirteen years.**

• **Bobby Cox became the ninth manager ever to win 2,000 games.**

Year: 2005   **Record: 90–72**

Second Place: Philadelphia Phillies, 88–74

Andruw Jones' Role: Set a team record with 51 homers

Notable:

• **The Braves played eighteen rookies at some point in the season while winning their fourteenth straight division title.**

The Braves' string of titles was one of the most impressive streaks of the regular-season accomplishments in any professional sport.

After struggling at the plate for most of 2001, Jones had ninth-inning homers on September 4 in Montreal and September 7 in Chicago to lift the Braves to 3–2 victories. He drove in 26 runs in 27 games beginning September 1.

While it may not have been as necessary in terms of bailing out his team, Jones' home-run binge in September 2002 was even more impressive. Before his 3-homer night, he became just the eleventh player in National League history to hit homers in four consecutive at-bats. He hit homers in his last two at-bats September 7 against the Montreal Expos and in his first two at-bats September 10 against the New York Mets.

The Mets had an early 5–0 lead before Jones homered to right with one out in the second inning. The lead was cut to 6–4 when Jones led off the fourth inning with a shot to left-center to tie the league record for consecutive homers. "I've been feeling good since we got back home from the last road trip," said Jones,

DID YOU KNOW?
The only previous Braves player to hit home runs in four consecutive at-bats was Bobby Lowe with the Boston Braves all the way back in 1894.

who added a 2-run single to lead the comeback to a 12–6 victory. "I'm just feeling good and I'm doing the right thing."[4]

SEPTEMBER TO REMEMBER

Andruw Jones' statistics for September 2002:

At-Bats:	78
Doubles:	8
Home Runs:	8
Runs Batted In:	18
Batting Average:	.359

ANOTHER STREAK

Jones carried the hot finish from 2002 into a fast start to the 2003 season. At the end of April, he started another hot streak. He had at least one RBI in nine straight games. The old team record of eight had been shared by Eddie Mathews (1954), Hank Aaron (1955, 1957), Mike Lum (1973), and Bob Horner (1979, 1980).

It did not take Jones long to make sure he broke the record. On May 8, 2003, Jones singled to drive in a run in the first inning, erasing the names of the four other players, including two Hall of Famers, from the top spot in the franchise record book.

Playing with baseball's biggest names at the All-Star Game, Jones had a double and home run in his two at-bats, driving in 3 runs and scoring twice. When the 2003 season was done, he had matched his best home-run total to date with 36 and reached a new high in RBIs with 116.

HELPING OTHERS

Andruw Jones and his wife, Nicole, serve as ambassadors for Jaden's Ladder.

"As a husband to Nicole and father of two, Druw Jr. and Madison, my family is the most important thing to me," Jones wrote on the Web site for the charitable organization, which addresses domestic-violence issues. "As with my family, I believe that all women and children deserve to feel safe and loved. That is why Jaden's Ladder is so important to me."

Jaden's Ladder helps women and children who have survived abusive situations. According to Jones, it strives to help them face their challenges and go on to more productive futures.

"It is my hope that, with my help and support, Jaden's Ladder will continue to make a difference—one woman, one child, one family at a time," Jones said.

Jaden's Ladder was founded in October 2004. While serving as one of the honorary directors of the nonprofit organization, Jones donates time and money to the annual fund-raiser. The organization hopes to provide victims with the opportunity to climb to new heights, breaking the cycle of domestic violence and becoming active members of the community.

Jones celebrates a home run against the Cincinnati Reds.

Jones' numbers dipped during the 2004 season. He was still one of the game's top outfielders, but he had not matched his own lofty standards. After batting .261 with 29 homers and 91 RBIs and setting a team record by striking out 147 times, Jones was committed to boosting his offensive performance for the 2005 season.

The best individual season was just ahead for Jones. His clutch Septembers and his continued defensive excellence even in what seemed like an "off" year for him in 2004 made him a major part of the streak of consecutive division titles that finally came to an end in 2006.

Jones and his Braves' teammates shared in an extended run of excellence. "I think the legacy is what it is," teammate Chipper Jones said. "We've won 14 straight. We know how special that is. We're going to keep doing our thing whether we win or lose in the postseason. It's not going to change the fact that we've won 14 straight division titles."[5]

> **"We're going to keep doing our thing whether we win or lose in the postseason."**
>
> **—Chipper Jones**

CHAPTER TEN

Baseball's Best

10

Andruw Jones was determined to make 2005 different. He brought a new batting stance and a new attitude with him to spring training.

One at-bat into the first exhibition game and Jones was already seeing the results. He hit a delivery from Los Angeles Dodgers pitcher Jeff Weaver over the fence in the first at-bat, then insisted his work was only beginning.

"You stay consistent and you're going to go far," Jones told reporters that day.[1] He knew one good at-bat in one exhibition game would ultimately be meaningless. Its only real purpose was to provide the first sign that there could be rewards ahead for a committed off-season.

When Jones was in the batting cage between the 2004 and 2005 seasons, he worked from a wider, more crouched stance. Hall of Famer Willie Mays had suggested the change to Jones, and the Braves staff agreed it was a good idea.

There was more, however, to the off-season commitment. Early in his career, Jones had been criticized for not always staying in the best condition in the off-season. He was known to come to spring training weighing a few more pounds and needing time to get into playing shape.

After feeling the disappointment of the increased strikeouts in 2004, Jones added more intensity to what had been an improving off-season routine. Teammate John Smoltz was often with Jones at those workouts. "I told people to watch what he was going to do," Smoltz said, "and I was right."[2]

As he reached his mid-twenties, Jones began arriving at spring training better prepared. Instead of being a player the team had to worry about in March, he became one the Braves could quickly see was ready to get started. After big springs in 2003 and 2004, Jones was unstoppable in 2005, batting .396 and hitting 10 home runs in 21 exhibition games.

"It seems like his whole demeanor has changed," home-run king and Braves executive vice president Hank Aaron said. "His approach is different—the way he wants to be depended on. He wants to set the

JONES' HOT STARTS IN SPRING TRAINING

YEAR	G	HR	RBI	AVG.
2003	21	3	13	.385
2004	25	4	8	.343
2005	21	10	21	.396

KEY:
G=Games
HR=Home Runs
RBI=Runs Batted In
AVG.=Average

example for the kids. He wants them to follow in his footsteps.

"I was never worried about Andruw's baseball ability. My concern was his approach to the game in the off-season. Sometimes kids spend too much time reading yesterday's news. What you do in baseball today has nothing to do with what you're going to do tomorrow. Baseball is a twelve-month game. Andruw is beginning to realize that."[3]

Jones' goal was to take off from his unbelievable spring and carry through with a consistent season-long performance. The realities of a 162-game season, however, are that every day players face ups and downs. They have hot streaks, but they must also endure slumps.

While Jones generally met his goal of a consistent performance, he did go through one slump. It was a big one, and it came in April, a time when it threatened to get his regular season off to a sour start. As the Braves traveled the country on a road trip from Philadelphia to Houston to Washington, Jones went

Jones walks away from the plate after striking out in the second inning against the Washington Nationals on April 21, 2006.

0-for-28 for the longest hitless streak of his career. "I think I was too anxious to have a great season," Jones said. "The team wasn't playing as well as we wanted. I was just trying to do too much. But I've always said the season is a marathon. It's not the way you start. It's the way you finish."[4]

Instead of letting that slump turn his season in the wrong direction, Jones steadily built up his batting average and his power numbers. Before long, it was clear he was headed to his best season ever.

There is no baseball franchise that epitomizes consistency more than the Braves. As the middle of the 2005 season approached, however, the team's streak of thirteen straight division titles seemed in jeopardy.

Jones was surrounded by rookies and other new teammates who had taken the places of injured players or those who had moved on to other teams. Jones became the man who made sure the streak reached fourteen seasons.

When he ripped 13 home runs in June, Jones set a team record for homers in a month. He was not finished. He hit 7 homers in regular-season games in July while also adding the second All-Star Game home run of his career.

Jones ripped 11 more homers and drove in 29 runs—nearly one a day—in August to become National League Player of the Month for the second time in three months. He is the only Brave to earn the award twice in one season.

DID YOU KNOW?

When Andruw Jones hit 13 home runs in June of 2005, he broke an Atlanta Braves team record that had stood for exactly fifty years. Eddie Mathews had held the team record for homers in a month with 12 in June 1955.

HOME-RUN RECORD

The extended summer hot streak led to a September assault on the team record book. Jones matched the franchise home-run record of 47 in

Chipper Jones (right) congratulates Andruw Jones on a 3-run home run against the Washington Nationals.

a season and then broke it September 11 when he sent an 0–1 pitch from Travis Hughes over the fence in left field in the third inning of a game in Washington. Jones' first homer of the night helped the Braves build an early 6–0 lead. After the Nationals rallied to tie, Chipper Jones and Andruw Jones hit back-to-back homers in the ninth inning to salvage a 9–7 win.

BRAVES' SINGLE-SEASON HOME-RUN LEADERS

Andruw Jones, 2005	51
Hank Aaron, 1971	47
Eddie Mathews, 1953	47
Eddie Mathews, 1959	46
Hank Aaron, 1962	45
Chipper Jones, 1999	45
Hank Aaron, 1957	44
Hank Aaron, 1963	44
Hank Aaron, 1966	44
Hank Aaron, 1969	44
Dale Murphy, 1987	44
Andres Galarraga, 1988	44

The 2-homer game put Jones on the brink of two milestones. He got there in impressive fashion three days later when he blasted a four hundred 434-foot shot off Geoff Geary in Philadelphia for his fiftieth homer of the season. It was also the three hundredth of his career, making Jones the fourth-youngest player in major-league history to get to that level.

"I've got the potential to hit home runs," Jones said.

HANK AARON AWARD WINNERS

YEAR	AMERICAN LEAGUE	NATIONAL LEAGUE
1999	Manny Ramirez	Sammy Sosa
2000	Carlos Delgado	Todd Helton
2001	Alex Rodriguez	Barry Bonds
2002	Alex Rodriguez	Barry Bonds
2003	Alex Rodriguez	Albert Pujols
2004	Manny Ramirez	Barry Bonds
2005	David Ortiz	Andruw Jones
2006	Derek Jeter	Ryan Howard

Jones rounds third base after hitting a 2-run home run against the New York Mets September 26, 2006.

"But I never go out there to hit a home run. I go out to hit the ball hard. I've got a natural swing lift with a little bit of an uppercut. That's the way my swing is."[5]

Jones' team-record total finished at 51 homers. He also led the National League with 128 RBIs.

Jones watches his home run against the Texas Rangers.

AWARD TIME?

Jones could no longer just be described as a wonderful defensive player who was also an explosive offensive weapon. His play in 2005 entered Jones' name into the debate about who was the best—and most valuable—player in baseball.

There were players from other teams who thought there was no reason to argue the point. In the six weeks that the Braves were without 1999 National League MVP Chipper Jones because of an injury, Andruw Jones held the offense together, batting .311 with 15 homers to gain the respect of opponents.

"I don't think there's really a race," Philadelphia Phillies reliever Billy Wagner said. "You've got a guy who's put this team on his back and is about to lead them into the playoffs again. Albert Pujols and Derek Lee, they've had great years, but when you look at what Jones had to protect him and playing with all the rookies, I think that what he's accomplished is worth him being the MVP."[6]

New York Mets outfielder Cliff Floyd agreed. "It's definitely him, even though D-Lee is one of my best friends and he and Pujols are having great years," Floyd said. "You're talking about a guy that had to carry a team with young guys around him while one of the other superstars was hurt."[7]

When it came time to add up the votes at award time, baseball fans and his fellow players declared

Jones' joy shows after he hit a solo home run against the Cubs May 28, 2006. The Braves hit a club-record eight homers in the 13–12 victory.

Jones as the best. He fell short, however, of the MVP award, which is given out by the Professional Baseball Writers of America Association.

Fan balloting led to the Hank Aaron Award, given to the best overall offensive player in each league. In the Players Choice Awards, voted by his peers, Jones was named Player of the Year and National League Outstanding Player.

Jones was thankful for the respect from opposing players. "I appreciate all the votes and all the players who selected me for these two awards," he said. "I especially want to thank my team that helped me produce every day and put up the numbers that I did."[8]

> **"I appreciate all the votes and all the players who selected me for these two awards."**
>
> **—Andruw Jones**

Baseball's record-setting home-run binge had slowed down, making Jones' season even more impressive. Nobody in Major League Baseball hit the 50-homer mark in 2003 or 2004, and he was the only one to get there in 2005. "It was one of the very best seasons I've ever seen anybody have," Braves general manager John Schuerholz said. "I can't imagine a guy having a fuller, more balanced, contributing kind of season for any team, anywhere."[9] In 2007, Jones signed a two-year contract with the Los Angeles Dodgers.

CAREER STATISTICS

Andruw Jones' career batting statistics

SEASON	G	AB	R	H	2B	3B
1996	31	106	11	23	7	1
1997	153	399	60	92	18	1
1998	159	582	89	158	33	8
1999	162	592	97	163	35	5
2000	161	656	122	199	36	6
2001	161	625	104	157	25	2
2002	154	560	91	148	34	0
2003	156	595	101	165	28	2
2004	154	570	85	149	34	4
2005	160	586	95	154	24	3
2006	156	565	107	148	29	0
2007	154	572	83	127	27	2
2008	75	209	21	33	8	1
Career	1,836	6,617	21	1,716	338	35

KEY:
G=Games
AB=At-Bats
R=Runs Scored
H=Hits
2B=Doubles
3B=Triples
HR=Home Runs

RBI=Runs Batted In
BB=Bases on Balls (Walks)
SO=Strikeouts
SB=Stolen Bases
CS=Caught Stealing
AVG.=Batting Average

HR	RBI	BB	SO	SB	CS	AVG.
5	13	7	29	3	0	.217
18	70	56	107	20	11	.231
31	90	40	129	27	4	.271
26	84	76	103	24	12	.275
36	104	59	100	21	6	.303
34	104	56	142	11	4	.251
35	94	83	135	8	3	.264
36	116	53	125	4	3	.277
29	91	71	147	6	6	.261
51	128	64	112	5	3	.263
41	129	82	127	4	1	.262
26	94	70	138	5	2	.222
3	14	27	76	0	1	.158
371	1,131	744	1,470	138	56	.259

CAREER ACHIEVEMENTS

1993	Signed first professional contract as sixteen-year-old.
1995–1996	Named Minor League Player of the Year, two times in a row, by *Baseball America*.
1996	Hit home runs in first two World Series at-bats and broke Mickey Mantle's record to become the youngest player ever to hit a homer in a World Series.
1998	Won the first of nine straight Gold Glove awards for his defensive play in the outfield.
2000	Played in All-Star Game for the first time.
2001	Selected for *Baseball America*'s 20th Anniversary Award of Excellence as the best minor-league player of the previous twenty years.

2005 Set Braves' record for home runs in a season with 51; led the National League in home runs (51) and RBIs (128); won his first Silver Slugger award as one of top three overall hitters among National League outfielders; received National League Hank Aaron Award as best overall player offensively.

CHAPTER NOTES

CHAPTER 1. WORLD SERIES DEBUT

1. Wayne Drehs, "Jones is a hero in his homeland," ESPN.com, <http://sports .espn.go.com/espn/print?id+2141626&type=story> (July 14, 2006).

2. Ibid.

3. Associated Press story from Cable News Network Web site, "Jones Steals Show in Opener," <http://members.tripod.com/~Bonbini/jones.htm> (July 14, 2006).

4. Associated Press story from *New York Times* Web site, "Curaçao Celebrates," <http://query.nytimes.com/gst/fullpage.html?res= 9407E6DF1030F937A15753C1A960958260> (July 14, 2006).

5. Associated Press story from Cable News Network Web site, "Jones Steals Show in Opener," <http://members.tripod.com/~Bonbini/jones.htm> (July 14, 2006).

6. Ibid.

7. Dave Kindred, "Nothing minor about Jones' talent," *The Sporting News*, <http://www.highbeam.com/library/docFree.asp?DOCID+1G1:18618747> (July 14, 2006).

8. Dave Anderson, "Jones is keeping up with some of baseball's biggest names," *New York Times*, <http://www.southcoasttoday.com/daily/ 10-96/10-22-96/d03sp157.htm> (July 14, 2006).

9. Associated Press story from Cable News Network Web site, "Jones Steals Show in Opener," <http://members.tripod.com/~Bonbini/jones.htm> (July 14, 2006).

CHAPTER 2. DARING TO DREAM

1. Wayne Drehs, "Jones is a hero in his homeland," ESPN.com, <http://sports .espn.go.com/espn/print?id+2141626&type=story> (July 14, 2006).

2. Sean Deveney, "Islander In The Sun – Andruw Jones of the Atlanta Braves," *The Sporting News*, October 9, 2000, <http://www.findarticles.com/p/ articles/mi_m1208/is_41_224/ai_66111257> (July 25, 2006).

3. Dave Anderson, "Jones is keeping up with some of baseball's biggest names," *New York Times*, <http://www.southcoasttoday.com/daily/ 10-96/10-22-96/d03sp157.htm> (July 14, 2006).

4. Ibid.

5. Ibid.

6. Sean Deveney, "Islander In The Sun – Andruw Jones of the Atlanta Braves," *The Sporting News*, October 9, 2000, <http://www.findarticles.com/p/articles/mi_m1208/is_41_224/ai_66111257> (July 25, 2006).

CHAPTER 3. ON THE WAY

1. Dave Anderson, "Jones is keeping up with some of baseball's biggest names," *New York Times*, <http://www.southcoasttoday.com/daily/10-96/10-22-96/d03sp157.htm> (July 14, 2006).

2. Royce Webb, "George Lombard interview," <http://www.sportsjones.com/lombard5.htm> (July 16, 2006).

3. *Baseball America*, Issue 0409, <http://www.baseball-almanac.com/players/player.php?p=jonesan01> (July 16, 2006).

4. Rich Radford, "There's Just No Keeping Up With This Jones: As He Rises in Braves' Ranks, So Does His Batting Average," *The Virginian-Pilot*, August 14, 1996, <http://scholar.lib.vt.edu/VA-news/VA-Piolt/issues/1996/vp960814/08140502.htm> (July 16, 2006).

CHAPTER 4. EARLY ARRIVAL

1. Rich Radford, "There's Just No Keeping Up With This Jones: As He Rises in Braves' Ranks, So Does His Batting Average," *The Virginian-Pilot*, August 14, 1996, <http://scholar.lib.vt.edu/VA-news/VAPiolt/issues/1996/vp960814/08140502.htm> (July 16, 2006).

2. Ibid.

3. Dave Anderson, "Jones is keeping up with some of baseball's biggest names," *New York Times*, <http://www.southcoasttoday.com/daily/10-96/10-22-96/d03sp157.htm> (July 14, 2006).

4. Steve Marantz, "In Jones and Dye, Atlanta has a rookie combination that could keep the Braves going … postseason after postseason after postseason," *The Sporting News*, <http://www.highbeam.com/library/docFree.asp?DOCID=1G1:18812185> (July 17, 2006).

5. Ibid.

CHAPTER 5. THERE TO STAY

1. Bob Nightengale, "Braves' bold move will haunt them," *The Sporting News*, April 7, 1997, <http://www.highbeam.com/library/docFree.asp?DOCID=1G1:19296060> (September 10, 2006).

CHAPTER 6. DEFENSIVE WHIZ

1. Sean Deveney, "Islander In The Sun – Andruw Jones of the Atlanta Braves," *The Sporting News*, October 9, 2000, <http://www.findarticles.com/p /articles/mi_m1208/is_41_224/ai_66111257> (July 25, 2006).

CHAPTER 7. EVERYDAY PLAYER

1. Sean Deveney, "Islander In The Sun – Andruw Jones of the Atlanta Braves," *The Sporting News*, October 9, 2000, <http://www.findarticles.com/p/ articles/mi_m1208/is_41_224/ai_66111257> (July 25, 2006).
2. Ibid.
3. Ibid.

CHAPTER 8. PLAYOFF UPSET

1. Jim Molony, "Braves sweep Astros out of playoffs," MLB.com, October 12, 2001, <http://mlb.mlb.com/NASApp/mlb/ws/news/ws_news_story_nl _1.jsp?article=10122001-1631> (September 10, 2006).
2. Sports Ticker story from *Sports Illustrated* Web site, "Atlanta Braves 1, Houston Astros 0," October 10, 2001, <http://sportsillustrated.cnn.com /baseball/mlb/nl/recaps/2001/10/10/astros_braves/> (September 10, 2006).
3. Mark Bowman, "Braves drop NLDS opener," MLB.com, October 6, 2004, <http://mlb.mlb.com/NASApp/mlb/atl/news/atl_gameday_recap.jsp?ymd=2 0041006&content_id=884935&vkey=recap&fext=.jsp> (August 5, 2006).

CHAPTER 9. CONTINUED DOMINANCE

1. Sports Ticker story on *USA Today* Web site, "Atlanta vs. Philadelphia," September 25, 2002, <http://www.usatoday.com/sports/scores102/ 102268/20020925NL---PHILADELPH0nr.htm> (September 10, 2006).
2. Ibid.
3. Ibid.
4. Sports Ticker story on *USA Today* Web site, "New York Mets vs. Atlanta," September 10, 2002, <http://www.usatoday.com/sports/scores102/ 102253/20020910NL---ATLANTA---0nr.htm> (September 6, 2006).
5. Mark Bowman, "Notes: LaRoche battles illness," MLB.com, October 9, 2005, <http://mlb.mlb.com/NASApp/mlb/news/article.jsp?ymd=20051009& content_id=1243761&vkey=news_atl&fext=.jsp&c_id=atl> (September 10, 2006).

CHAPTER 10. BASEBALL'S BEST

1. Travis Haney, Morris News Service, "Jones top candidate for MVP," *Athens Banner-Herald*, September 19, 2005, <http://onlineathens.com/stories /092005/spo_20050920051.shtml> (September 6, 2006).

2. Ibid.

3. Jeff Schultz, "Aaron singing the praises of A. Jones," *Atlanta Journal-Constitution* Web site blog, August 18, 2005, <http://www.ajc.com /blogs/content/shared-blogs/ajc/sportscolumns/entries/2005/08/18/aaron _singing_t.html> (September 10, 2006).

4. Mark Bowman, "Andruw a dual Players Choice Winner," MLB.com, November 3, 2005, <http://mlbplayers.mlb.com/NASApp/mlb/news/article .jsp?ymd+20051102&content_id+1263836.jsp> (September 8, 2006).

5. Ibid.

6. Travis Haney, Morris News Service, "Jones top candidate for MVP," *Athens Banner-Herald*, September 19, 2005, <http://onlineathens.com/stories/ 092005/spo_20050920051.shtml> (September 6, 2006).

7. Ibid.

8. Mark Bowman, "Andruw a dual Players Choice Winner," MLB.com, November 3, 2005, <http://mlbplayers.mlb.com/NASApp/mlb/news/article .jsp?ymd+20051102&content_id+1263836.jsp> (September 8, 2006).

9. Mark Bowman, "Andruw named NL Aaron Award winner," October 26, 2005, <http://mlb.mlb.com/NASApp/mlb/news/article.jsp?ymd+20051026& content_id=1260018&vkey=ps2005news&fext+.jsp> (September 6, 2006).

GLOSSARY

charity—The act of giving or an organization that gives to the needy.

error—A misplay on defense that allows a batter to be safe or a runner to advance to another base.

farm system—The use by Major League Baseball teams of lower-level teams designed to develop talent.

Gold Glove—An award that goes to the best defensive player at each position in each league for the year.

manager—The head coach of a professional baseball team.

prospect—An athlete who is believed to have the potential to perform on a higher level.

range factor—A statistical measure of the number of plays a defensive player makes in a typical game.

rookie—A first-year professional.

scout—A person who evaluates baseball players to help teams determine who to draft and/or sign to contracts.

spring training—When baseball teams travel to Florida or Arizona to prepare for an upcoming season.

World Series—A series of between four and seven games, matching the American League and National League baseball champions. The first team to win four games is declared world champion.

FOR MORE INFORMATION

WEB LINKS

Jaden's Ladder:
www.jadensladder.org

Jones' page on MLB.com:
http://losangeles.dodgers.mlb.com/team/
          player.jsp?player_id=116662

Jones' page on ESPN Web site:
http://sports.espn.go.com/mlb/players/profile?statsId=5681

Jones' page on Baseball-Reference.com:
http://www.baseball-reference.com/j/jonesan01.shtml

INDEX

W